AWARD WINNING AUTHOR
MARTIE SMITH

BATTLING CONFUSION WITH INNOVATION

CREATIVE CHAOS WARRIOR

ISBN: 978-1-964619-25-5

Introduction

Creative Chaos Warrior is your companion on the journey of embracing life's ups and downs and turning them into a source of strength and creativity. Written by the talented and award-winning author Martie Smith, this book is packed with real-life stories, practical advice, and steps you can take to find resilience in the face of chaos.

Whether you're going through tough times or just looking to tap into your creative side, *Creative Chaos Warrior* is here to guide you. It's more than just a book—it's a roadmap to help you harness the chaos around you and turn it into something positive and empowering.

Dive in, join a community of like-minded warriors, and learn how to not just survive in chaos but to truly thrive.

Table of Contents

CHAPTER 1

Becoming an Innovative
Warrior of Chaos

Did you ever face a chaotic event that froze you with anxiety and stress - a situation where you were left wondering how to resolve it? Did you find yourself questioning what you needed to do to overcome obstacles?

I want to introduce a fantastic finding I made and invite you to plunge into the extraordinary world of becoming a Creative Chaos Warrior. The purpose of this book is to unveil the secrets of mastering creativity when chaos emerges in your life. By exploring the essence of imagination, appreciating the art of disruption, and gaining the weapons necessary for creative conquest, I will show you the transformative journey that unleashed my creative potential.

From wielding a Sword of Innovation to harnessing the Shield of Resilience, each chapter will equip you as an aspiring warrior with the tools, weapons, and mindset needed to thrive in the ever-changing landscape of creativity as it has in my life. Joining the ranks of the Creative Chaos Warriors and launching yourself on a quest to unlock your inventive powers, conquer challenges, and forge new paths in artistic expression is mind-blowing and worth the experience.

Becoming an innovative warrior of chaos is undoubtedly one of my most rewarding decisions. It made me persistent, knowledgeable, and able to express myself via my story while encouraging others that they can do more than they think. You must be conscious of who you are, where you have been, and how, traversing your life's path, you have acquired much more than you were aware of.

First, let me break down the pros of becoming a Creative Chaos Warrior and weigh the importance of embracing this path. You ultimately decide if it's a fit worth considering.

You will become an innovative thinker, allowing creativity to respond during chaos by thinking outside normal boundaries. You will foster innovative solutions to complex problems, essential in adapting to changing environments, driving progress, and staying aware. A Creative Chaos Warrior can bring fresh perspectives that lead to breakthroughs and advancements, making them invaluable assets in today's fast-paced world.

As a Creative Chaos Warrior, you will excel at surfing through uncertainty and thrive in dynamic situations. By embracing chaos, you will develop adaptability skills crucial for success in an ever-evolving world. The ability to pivot quickly, adjust strategies, and find opportunities in chaos is an essential strsength for you as a warrior, enabling you to stay resilient and relevant in tumultuous times.

Once you embark on the journey of a Creative Chaos Warrior, you must have the courage to step into the unknown and build resilience to overcome challenges. These qualities are fundamental for growth, empowering you to confront fears, take risks, and bounce back from failures. By embracing chaos with courage and resilience, you inspire others to face uncertainty with confidence and determination, traversing a world of innovation and progress.

The path of a Creative Chaos Warrior is one of continuous learning and development. You will expand your knowledge, skills, perspectives, personal development, and adaptability by greeting chaos and exploring new possibilities. A Creative Chaos Warrior is a lifelong learner who can thrive on challenges, seek new experiences, and cultivate a growth attitude that propels you forward in your quest for self-improvement and excellence.

The pros of becoming a Creative Chaos Warrior underscore the importance of embracing creativity, adaptability, courage, inspiration, and continuous learning in deciphering complexity, driving innovation, and achieving success in a rapidly changing world. While the path may be challenging, the rewards of becoming a warrior are substantial, allowing you to make a lasting impact, inspire others, and thrive in uncertainty.

Confronting chaos can be a thrilling and rewarding experience, but it also entails traveling through an environment of risk and uncertainty. While this can be overwhelming for some, it can lead to incredible growth and learning opportunities. Constantly dealing with chaos and unpredictability can be challenging and tiring, and a Creative Chaos Warrior must prioritize self-care and relaxation. You can continue to prosper in your adventurous spirit by maintaining a healthy balance.

Not everyone will immediately understand or appreciate the approach of a Creative Chaos Warrior. However, by communicating effectively and building understanding and support, you can work to overcome any resistance or pushback you may encounter. The approach, without fear or doubt, kept me interested in finding solutions. It was a game-changer. Here are some reasons why adopting this role is not only beneficial but also empowering, like it was for me:

- Becoming a Creative Chaos Warrior is a path filled with challenges and options. It requires embracing ambiguity, thinking outside the box, and taking risks while remaining adaptable and resilient to uncertainty. By embodying these qualities, you can drive innovation, inspire others, and continually learn and grow. While it may not be for everyone, those who embrace the chaos may find themselves on a rewarding and fulfilling personal and professional development journey.

- In today's constantly changing world, being innovative and becoming creative allows you to quickly adapt to new situations and easily learn to triumph in any unpredictable environment. Confronting chaos will stimulate your creativity and prompt you to think differently. You will be looking at and thinking about solutions vs problems. You shall learn to experiment with ingenious solutions and find feasible answers to problems. You may even become a visionary who motivates others to exceed their limits and achieve a better approach during mayhem.

I invite you to join me on this exhilarating journey to becoming a Creative Chaos Warrior. This approach challenges conventional thinking and empowers you, as a reader, to redefine your creativity in the face of uncertainty.

Through its dynamic chapters, this book will take you on a quest to surpass your limitations, welcome the unpredictable, and wield unconventional tools for unleashing your creative prowess. You will adopt the Art of Disruption while crafting your unique Innovation Arsenal.

Each chapter will motivate you to break free from traditional boundaries. You will pave a new path towards imaginative distinction. Join the ranks of leaders and daring innovators as you go on this epic odyssey of self-discovery and limitless creativity.

By confronting chaos directly, you develop resilience and learn to overcome setbacks, failures, and unexpected events with renewed strength and determination. You may even become unstoppable and unbreakable.

Chaos helped me identify opportunities where, before, I only saw disorder. I am becoming a master of opportunity, always one step ahead of the game. I am much more aware of the bigger picture and alert. Thinking is one of the benefits of these situations.

This book emphasizes the importance of resilience in navigating circumstances. Through stories of perseverance, adaptability, overcoming setbacks, and loads of faith, readers discover resilience is fundamental for thriving in chaotic environments and leveraging adversity as a springboard for creative growth. Becoming a Creative Chaos Warrior inspires you to break free from limiting beliefs, embrace ambiguity, and cultivate a mindset that views chaos as a powerful force for unleashing untapped potential and igniting innovative thinking.

You will explore a world where creativity knows no limits and chaos sparks invention. Embrace the unexpected, challenge the normal situation, and convert ideas into bold creations. Become a fearless, Creative Chaos Warrior and conquer the extent of artistry with passion and authenticity. Unleash your inventive potential and forge new paths in the ever-evolving landscape of your imagination.

You may even form a community of like-minded individuals exploring creativity, innovation, and artistic expression. Discover your unique path to creative mastery. Are you willing to take on an epic journey of artistic adventure?

You will also draw courage, strength, and many other qualities that will arm you with the arsenal to have the right stuff to handle uncertainty during chaos. These qualities can help you become a creative chaos warrior by providing a solid foundation for navigating through uncertainty, embracing challenges, and fostering innovative thinking. Here's how each quality can contribute to your quest:

- Resilience allows you to be a creative chaos warrior and bounce back from setbacks, failures, or unexpected circumstances. It enables you to focus and commit to actualizing your goals.

- Compassion toward others fosters strong relationships, collaboration, and understanding, which are essential in chaotic scenarios where teamwork and empathy play crucial roles.

- Critical thinking and problem-solving skills become vital in chaotic situations. Your intelligence enables you, as a creative chaos warrior, to analyze complex problems, find innovative solutions, and adapt to changing circumstances effectively.

- Courage helps individuals take risks, explore new ideas, and escape familiar zones. It allows individuals to face uncertainty confidently and embrace challenges as opportunities for wisdom and growth.

- Self-confidence and empowerment are vital in motivating oneself to overcome obstacles, take initiative, and drive positive change in chaotic environments. You will gain the ability to adapt quickly to changing conditions and unforeseen challenges, which is essential for dealing with chaos and staying agile in dynamic situations.

- Creative thinking is at the core of being a Chaos Warrior. It enables individuals to see problems from different perspectives, think decisively, and develop innovative solutions in uncertainty.

- Leadership skills can help you inspire and influence others, encourage collaboration, and steer a team toward a common goal, even in turbulent times.

- Authenticity allows Creative Chaos Warriors to stay true to their values, express their unique ideas, and bring their genuine selves to the table, applying creativity and originality. Treating oneself and others respectfully creates a positive support system that encourages open communication, trust, and mutual understanding, all essential elements in chaotic situations.

Are you ready to be a chaos warrior and revolutionize the world around you? Let's infuse some excitement and inspiration into becoming an innovator as a Creative Chaos Warrior, join an exciting course in life, and gain personal growth.

CHAPTER 2

Facing Turmoil? Hang in There

I want to provide you and humanity with a well-thought-out and inspiring message about combatting chaos and becoming a warrior to diffuse obstacles, disorder, and confusion in today's hectic world environment.

In the battlefield of life today, chaos often reigns supreme, thrusting you into turmoil and uncertainty. The true warrior within me can emerge during these moments of upheaval. This warrior is not defined solely by brute force or combat skills but by an invincible spirit, a beacon of courage, resilience, and determination.

You will combat chaos and emerge victorious when you apply the knowledge, I have been blessed with. It helps to embrace your inner warrior with a beacon of courage, resilience, and determination to gain victory over chaotic turmoil. Still, it takes homework, practice, perseverance, strategies, determination, discernment, support, and seeing the situation in full context to win.

With its unpredictable nature, chaos can disorient and overwhelm you and me. Yet, the seeds of growth and transformation are sown within this chaos. A warrior will understand that chaos is not the enemy. You can welcome it as a formidable adversary to be faced head-on. Instead of succumbing to fear and doubt, a warrior harnesses chaos as fuel for inner strength and resolve.

Adversity will temper your warrior's spirit, forging resilience and fortitude in the fires of struggle. Every trial and tribulation will become an opportunity for growth and self-discovery. Like a sword being sharpened on the whetstone of adversity, you emerge as a warrior capable and resilient with each challenge you learn to overcome.

Fear is a natural response to chaos, but a warrior does not allow fear to dictate actions. Instead, you cultivate courage, and you face your fears with relentless determination. It is through courage that you, as a warrior, transcend your limitations and embrace your true potential. So, know that courage is key in the face of fear.

Imagine a scenario where chaos surrounds you—perhaps a personal crisis, a sudden loss, or a challenging situation at work. How do you navigate such turmoil and emerge stronger on the other side? Let's delve into the lessons I've learned from mentors about facing limiting beliefs and embracing the mindset of a warrior in the thick of chaos.

One of my crises was the thought of using a wheelchair. That turmoil turned my life upside down, leaving me disoriented and desperate. Both characteristics tend toward loss and not thinking clearly. But now I see it as adapting and learning to be compassionate, a reminder to be grateful my limbs were still part of me, just not fully functional.

To combat chaos and emerge victorious, I knew I must cultivate the mindset of a warrior. This mindset manifests with courage, resilience, and a relentless determination to overcome obstacles. It's about embracing challenges as opportunities for personal growth and transformation and learning alternatives to my narrow-minded approach to resolving problems.

I've encountered moments of turmoil where my own limiting beliefs threatened to overwhelm me, frozen with doubt, fear, and disastrous thoughts. My past experiences or societal conditioning, which I had absorbed, instilled these beliefs. I learned that those limited ideas would hinder my progress and build resilience.

However, through the guidance of my mentors and personal reflection, I learned to identify and challenge these limiting beliefs. I began to remodel those ideas with opportunities or options. Instead of facing insurmountable obstacles, I felt were unconquerable before.

My mentors played a crucial role in helping me confront and overcome limiting beliefs. They provided guidance, wisdom, and encouragement during challenging times, especially during the strain of the pandemic. I was fortunate to have mentors who taught me valuable lessons about resilience and perseverance in the face of chaos. They were energetic, invincible, and unstoppable, and I wanted to follow their example of approaching problems or setbacks with a can-do attitude. I wanted that.

One important lesson is the power of self-awareness. By recognizing your limiting beliefs—such as "I'm not good enough" or "I can't handle this"—you can begin to dismantle them. Mentors have taught me to question my limiting beliefs and think with more positivity and confidence-building thoughts and affirmations. I started to see the roadblocks that my limiting beliefs would produce. They are simply speedbumps I have learned to ride over without stopping or crashing and losing control of my approach.

They also inspired me to list my limiting beliefs. Writing them down revealed patterns of what I thought and felt, always tending to be pessimistic. I began addressing emotions head-on. What were my feelings or emotions? Were they negative ones that would lead me to always think about failure? Or were they bound by positivity and motivation in my approach to overcoming the mayhem?

I started leaving a lot of negativities behind. I was discovering patterns repeated with similar thoughts of unworthiness and wanting to suppress my emotions. I began adding the possibility that it may work. I traded it in the dread for let's give it a try.

The warrior's journey involves turning adversity into strength. Every trial and tribulation becomes an opportunity for growth and self-discovery. Just as a sword is tempered in the fires of adversity, so are we strengthened through challenges.

When faced with chaos, it's natural to experience fear and doubt. However, a warrior does not allow fear to dictate actions. Instead, you cultivate courage and face your fears with determination. This courage is essential for transcending limiting beliefs and embracing your true potential.

Persistence and resilience are the hallmarks of my warrior's spirit. I do not give up in the face of challenges, but I am determined. Every setback becomes a bridge towards victory.

Mentors have taught me the importance of perseverance in overcoming obstacles. They've shared stories of their struggles and triumphs, inspiring me to keep pushing forward even when the road ahead seems daunting.

No warrior fights alone. Unity and support from like-minded individuals are essential for navigating through chaos. Mentors have emphasized the importance of forging strong bonds with others and creating a network of support and collaboration.

By collaborating with others and seeking guidance from mentors, you gain strength and resilience in the face of chaos. Together, we can overcome challenges that would be insurmountable on our own. You can eradicate turmoil and advance on your path to achieving freedom.

A vital aspect of the warrior's mindset is harnessing inner strength. This inner strength comes from self-awareness, mindfulness, and a steadfast belief in our abilities. Mentors have taught me to draw from this vital wellspring of inner strength, enabling me to confront chaos with unwavering conviction and tenacity.

It is essential to resort to your inner reservoir of resilience and determination in moments of turmoil. This inner strength empowers you to face challenges and navigate through chaos with grace and grit.

Courage is the cornerstone of the warrior's mindset. It's about facing fears and uncertainties with bravery and resolve. Mentors have encouraged me to cultivate courage in adversity, reminding me that true strength lies in confronting challenges with an open heart and a fearless spirit.

By embracing courage, we transcend our limitations and unlock our true potential. We learn to navigate through chaos confidently and poise, knowing we have the inner fortitude to overcome any obstacle.

Perseverance is the power that propels us forward on the warrior's journey. It means staying committed to your goals and realizing your dreams despite setbacks and challenges. Mentors have taught me the importance of persistence, emphasizing that every small step counts towards achieving our objectives.

Perseverance keeps us focused and determined in times of turmoil. It enables us to weather the storm and emerge stronger on the other side. With perseverance, we turn chaos into an opportunity for growth and transformation.

In conclusion, facing turmoil requires embracing the mindset of a warrior—courageous, resilient, and determined. Mentors are vital in guiding us through challenging times, helping us confront limiting beliefs, and empowering us to turn adversity into strength.

As you navigate through life's chaos, remember to hang in there and practice the lessons from mentors. Challenge your limiting beliefs, cultivate courage and resilience, and seek support from those around you. Embrace your inner warrior and emerge victorious on the battlefield of life. With perseverance and resilience, you can overcome any obstacle and thrive amidst chaos.

Harness your inner strength, embrace courage, and embody perseverance. Let your warrior spirit guide you through the challenges that life throws your way. Remember, you have the power within you to conquer chaos and emerge more vital than ever before. Embrace the journey, embrace the warrior within, and seize every opportunity for growth and transformation. You are able, you are resilient, and you are also destined for greatness. So, hang in there and let your warrior spirit shine!

Are you ready to become a creative chaos warrior? Let me share some fantastic techniques and practices that can inspire and motivate you to navigate life's challenges with resilience, determination, courage, and self-care.

First, we have resilience techniques, such as mindset reframing and visualization. These can help you view challenges as opportunities for growth and picture yourself triumphing over difficulties with courage and resilience.

Next, we have determination strategies that include goal-setting and action plans. These can help you break down your tasks into manageable steps and build momentum to advance with larger objectives, no matter how chaotic your life may get.

We also have courage-building practices, such as gradually facing fears and self-affirmations, that can help you grow stronger and more confident.

Of course, we must remember the importance of balancing chaos with self-care. Time management techniques like priority setting, time blocking, and boundary-setting strategies like saying no and digital detox can help you prioritize your well-being amidst life's chaos.

Self-compassion practices like gratitude journaling, kindness to self, and seeking support and connection can also help you nurture your inner self and maintain emotional balance.

Embracing imperfection and growth is also critical to being a creative chaos warrior. By embracing mistakes, staying flexible and adaptable, and celebrating small wins, you can continuously evolve into a stronger and more resilient version of yourself.

So, are you ready to embrace your imperfections, face challenges head-on, and continuously evolve into a creative chaos warrior? You've got this!

Here are some handy things that you can utilize in your battles to become a Creative Chaos Warrior:

Specific Tools and Weapons:

Resilience Techniques:

- **Mindset Reframing:** Reframe your setbacks or adversities as learning opportunities, emphasizing them as personal growth and adaptation.
- **Visualization:** Visualization exercises where you imagine and see overcoming challenges with resilience and determination.

Determination Strategies:

- **Goal Setting:** Set specific, achievable goals even amidst chaos, fostering a sense of purpose and direction.
- **Action Plans:** Create actionable plans to tackle obstacles step by step, maintaining focus and motivation. Go at your own pace.

Courage Building Practices:

- **Facing Fears Gradually:** Gradual exposure to fears or challenges builds self-confidence.
- **Self-Affirmations:** Positive affirmations help boost self-belief and courage during turbulent times.

Balancing Chaos with Self-Care:

Time Management Techniques:

- **Priority Setting:** Identify and prioritize tasks amidst chaos and focus on what truly matters.
- **Time Blocking:** Teach yourself to allocate dedicated time slots for self-care activities, ensuring they are noticed

Boundary-Setting Strategies:

- **Saying No:** Set healthy boundaries by politely declining non-essential commitments. Establish your limits honestly with others.
- **Digital Detox:** Periodically unplugging from technology to reduce overwhelm and promote relaxation will improve your decision-making and resolve turmoil.

Self-Compassion Practices:

- **Mindful Awareness:** Mindfulness exercises help you stay present and non-judgmental amidst chaos.
- **Self-Care Rituals:** Regular self-care rituals such as prayer, meditation, exercise, or journaling to nurture emotional and spiritual well-being.

Building Understanding and Support:

Effective Communication Methods:

- **Storytelling:** Sharing your personal stories to convey the Creative Chaos Warrior approach authentically and relatably will give you more compassion.

- **Active Listening:** Teach yourself active listening skills to nurture deeper connections and empathy with others.

Forming Community Engagement Strategies:

- **Seeking Allies:** Identifying supportive individuals or your tribe who resonate with an innovative mindset.
- **Networking:** Participation in community events or forums builds relationships and exchanges ideas to better respond to adversity.

Inclusive Leadership Approaches:

- **Lead by Example:** Live to exemplify the Creative Chaos Warrior mindset in their interactions, inspiring others through action.
- **Empowering Others:** Advocate for empowering others to embrace creativity and adaptability, fostering a collective sense of purpose and resilience.

CHAPTER 3

Armed with a Sword of Resilience and a Shield of Love

Learning to welcome chaos as a catalyst for creativity and personal growth will convert you into a Creative Chaos Warrior. But it would be best if you were armed to confront a struggle like anyone facing a battle. Now, my weapons of choice that never fail me are my Sword of Resilience and the Shield of Love.

A warrior must be armed. But things change when you use a Sword of Resilience to wade through chaos. Why? Because resilience is the ability to withstand and recover from difficult situations. In the face of turmoil, having resilience allows you, as a warrior, to stay strong, adapt to changing circumstances, and persevere despite challenges. As a sturdy sword can cut through obstacles, resilience enables you to ride through turbulent times, maintain focus, and emerge stronger on the other side.

Resilience is a sturdy sword for me that I now carry in battles. It has allowed me to adapt to unexpected situations and adjust my strategies. Just like a sharp blade can be wielded in different ways, my Sword of Resilience will enable me to be flexible and respond effectively to changing circumstances. It teaches me to adapt and adjust my plan to conquer challenges.

That sword gives me the strength and tolerance to endure trials without giving up. It is durable and can withstand brutal blows. It helps me persevere through difficult times, keep moving forward, and find solutions.

In chaotic conditions, my emotions do run high. Resilience also helps me manage emotions, stay calm under pressure, and make rational decisions with more clarity. That emotional strength is akin to the sharpness of a sword, allowing for precision and control. It cut through the meat of the problem. It chops down the plan into mini-tasks that make the goals more attainable.

Even if I face setbacks or failures, that Sword of Resilience enables me to bounce back and recover quickly. Like a well-maintained knife that can be sharpened and polished, resilience allows me to learn from my mistakes, grow more robust, and continue the fight. It will enable me to progress forward with strength and drive.

By wielding my Sword of Resilience, I can navigate chaos's unpredictable and tumultuous nature. Once I wade through the armed forces to win the challenge, I am stronger and more capable on the other side.

In the last few years, I have learned to apply practical strategies for adapting to new circumstances. I am also finding opportunities for innovation amid the chaotic influx in this world recently. This approach has proven effective in deciphering how to handle the bombardment of confusion that the world has thrown at me lately.

Hope is present in the chaotic sphere where uncertainty dominates, and challenges lurk around every corner. A rare breed of warriors I was privileged to have met in my adventurous life exists. I dubbed these individuals Creative Chaos Warriors. These warriors were mentors and experts in empowerment who taught me to harness the power of love and resilience. I witnessed them negotiating the ever-shifting landscapes of their chaotic world. But they had the resilience to overcome adversity. They became my inspiration as I absorbed the handy tips they shared.

I had yet to acknowledge the wisdom they were sharing back then. I now see what I couldn't see then. My self-induced chaos clouded my judgment. In retrospect, I now know there is always an unleashed, perhaps transformative, power of knowledge and truth within you.

Somehow, being in a blinding fog limited me from all these resources. But now I share with you what I have learned. Those troopers and those lessons gave me a hunger to read, to discover awe and love. It gave me a chance to be a creative soul. All pure blessings from God and that word of "Resilience" were handed to me by God. He was giving me a weapon that would give me the grace to deal with things, unlike before. What that taught me were resourceful and creative gold nuggets that transformed me into a warrior. It taught me what l now want to share with the world.

I, Martie M. Smith, now declare I have become a seasoned, Creative Chaos Warrior thanks to those mentors and the treasure of knowledge. I am now venturing into the unknown with firm faith, prepared to battle uncertainty with these weapons protecting me from going into the swirl of mayhem. I now carry a steadfast light of truth within my heart, wearing a Shield of Love to protect me.

This love fueled my interactions with the fellow warriors I encountered. They formed nurturing bonds of trust and unbreakable camaraderie in the face of adversity. Amid that chaos, that love now whispers words of encouragement and compassion, guiding me through the darkest times. It was when God showed me how to love myself and deliver a legacy of hope, branding my Sword of Resilience and wearing my Shield of Love.

But that love was not enough to sustain me early on in my journey. This dimension of Creative Chaos demanded conquering fear, stubborn resilience, and a warrior's grit that could weather the fiercest storms. With each challenge I encounter, I call upon my inner strength, refusing to be defeated by the chaotic forces that used to seek to derail my quest to conquer the upheaval and uncertainty. My ability to bounce back is more present than ever, and I am no longer paralyzed in fear and doubt.

The Sword of Resilience and the Shield of Love continue to form a formidable alliance within me, shaping me into a warrior of unparalleled courage and determination. In the heat of battles, when all seemed lost, that power of love ignited a fire within my soul, propelling me forward with a committed purpose. And when faced with insurmountable odds, resilience has always stood as a weapon of strength, reminding me of my now invincible spirit. These things were revealed only when I opened my mind, heart, and soul to the truth. It is what caused my epic transformation.

Through the trials and tribulations of my journey, I learned that the true essence of a Creative Chaos Warrior lies not in the chaos itself but in the way you navigate its tumultuous waters. Wearing my Shield of love is akin to a compass responding to disorder and the Sword of Resilience that helps me forge ahead, carving a path of light and hope amidst the shadows of unpredictability.

And so, as I, Martie Smith, the Creative Chaos Warrior, now march onward, a beacon of love and resilience in a world teetering on the brink of disorder. With every step I take, I embrace the power of my virtues, knowing they will lead me to ultimate fulfillment and strength in the face of chaos. As I evolve and stride forward, the world around me seems to bend and twist, reshaping itself in response to my boundless imagination and creativity.

I continue to learn a great deal about mastering chaos. I now weave beauty from all that discord and find harmony in the most unlikely places. My gratitude for the many blessings I discovered has paved that incredible path for me. Now, my mission is to pay it forward and share tips on how I mastered this.

The Lord handed me another weapon for this warrior on the battlefield of ideas. My creativity is like a Sword of Innovation, cutting through doubt and fear with each stroke. I now accept the unpredictable nature of the creative process, seeing chaos not as an obstacle but more as a canvas upon which to paint my dreams into reality.

So, to those of you who dare to embrace the chaos, to you who seek a spark of inspiration within yourselves, take heart in the examples I share with you of how becoming a Creative Chaos Warrior can rid you of unwarranted fear and confusion and how it can train you to respond with clarity and conviction. Let my story be a beacon of light in the darkness, a reminder that within every storm lies the potential for beauty and growth within every challenge within your existing powers (you may not have been aware that they exist, as it happened to me).

My willingness to share my story and inspire others took tremendous courage and vulnerability. My journey from feeling alone and rejected to finding acceptance and purpose is a testament to the inner strength and resilience I possess, and you have the potential to harness and thrive as well.

Embracing your unique path and focusing on your passion and purpose, rather than external expectations, is a profound realization that I am grateful for beyond words. My journey reminds me that you can shape your destiny and find meaning in facing challenges and actions, even if you can't see the light in the tunnel.

As I continue to seize my role as a Creative Chaos Warrior, I want to inspire you to find inner strength, resilience, and faith. Your story can become a beacon of hope and empowerment, showing that overcoming obstacles and finding purpose in the middle of chaos is possible, as it was for me. My experiences have cultivated a deep well of wisdom and empathy, allowing me to connect with others profoundly.

This journey of self-discovery and growth has given me a unique perspective on life that is powerful and transformative. As I navigate through the ever-changing landscape of my life, I remember the lessons learned along the way. I accept any disorder as a catalyst for creativity and growth, knowing that my ability to adapt and prosper in uncertainty is a testament to my resilience and that God has taught me to overcome it.

This book reminds us that our past does not define us but shapes us into the unique individuals we can become. Your willingness to share your vulnerabilities and triumphs is a gift to those around you, inspiring them to embrace their journeys with courage and grace.

As a Creative Chaos Warrior, you will possess a rare blend of strength, flexibility, and compassion that sets you apart. Embrace this role with confidence and authenticity, knowing that your unique perspective can inspire and uplift others in their paths. Keep shining your light brightly, and let that Creative Chaos Warrior spirit guide you through life's twists and turns with grace and resilience. Turn your story into a testament to the power of perseverance, faith, and self-discovery.

During the chaos and mayhem, remember that you possess an indomitable inner strength that can withstand even the wildest storm. Be ready to boldly ride the turbulent currents, knowing you can overcome any challenge. Please take a moment to acknowledge your emotions without judgment; they testify to your humanity and validity. Let these emotions guide you through the labyrinth of uncertainty with resilience and grace. Yes, it's time to get real courage and be vulnerable. Confront those feelings that rush forth at you and enter battles of confusion. Because if you skip all that, you won't be able to see, trust me.

As you enter that battlefield of confusion, you will wear your Shield of Resilience with unyielding determination. Let its blade represent your unbreakable spirit, ready to slice through the shadows of doubt and fear. With every swing, reclaim your power and assert your presence during turmoil. Trust in your faith in God and yourself. Recognize your divine ability to rise above the chaos, knowing that every strike makes you stronger and more resilient. Knowing that God is arming you with tools you never knew you had.

CHAPTER 4

Finding Balance Amidst Chaos

I used to ask this when an insurmountable obstacle appeared before me: "Martie, what the hell are you going to do? Oh, forget it. You're all over the map, every which way but unknown." Whenever chaotic situations happened, I wanted to lose it. I had no sure grip on anything happening and got confused. I didn't know where to turn; I didn't know whom to talk to. That was my typical response. I was oblivious to the well of wisdom that could gush forth, using creativity as the driving force to get me through the disruption of my clarity.

In moments of chaos, my instincts lead me astray, pushing toward exaggeration and clouding my ability to see potential solutions. It's natural to feel overwhelmed and seek comfort in avoidance, but I learned that your actual growth and evolution come from facing those fears head-on.

To navigate chaos effectively, it is crucial to maintain a **firm belief in yourself and your ability to respond.** You should trust your instincts and listen to your gut. They will guide you away from reactive impulses and towards thoughtful, measured actions and responses. Instead of succumbing to panic and confusion, take a step back and look at the situation differently. Examine the situation objectively, identifying the root causes of disorganization and stress. By doing so, you will identify viable solutions and overcome the obstacles and presumed impossibility of conquering challenges.

By **acknowledging the reality** of the circumstances and understanding their true impact, you can begin to regain control. Separate what directly affects you from what doesn't. While it's essential to be concerned about broader issues, it's equally crucial to prioritize your mental and emotional well-being. Focus on what you can control and let go of what lies beyond your influence. It would help if you created balance or stability to maneuver better.

Accepting responsibility for what is yours to bear empowers you to respond effectively. When you assume responsibility for things beyond your control, you invite chaos into your life. It becomes challenging to distinguish between what truly matters and what is merely a distraction. You'll find clarity amid that turmoil by recognizing your limits and focusing on what you can change.

The root causes of my distress were identified by the moments when I felt most vulnerable and lost in the chaos. This warrior-to-be began with those moments as a starting point for my introspection. What was causing me to feel overwhelmed? Were external factors beyond my control or my internal turmoil magnifying the situation? Was it my thoughts, beliefs, or emotions? What was causing an imbalance?

With each question posed, I felt a glimmer of clarity emerge from the fog of my confusion. It wasn't easy **confronting my numerous fears and doubts head-on**, but now I know it was necessary to break free from the cycle of chaos that threatened to engulf me. That chaos, which only saw pain instead of enduring suffering, would teach me to defend my heart with love, not fear.

Taking a deep breath, I consciously began owning responsibility for myself. I finally started recognizing that while I couldn't control every external factor, I had the power to control how I responded to them. It was a liberating realization that empowered me to take charge of my narrative and shape my reality in a way that aligned with my instilled values and beliefs.

Armed with this newfound sense of clarity and purpose, I set out to untangle the knots of confusion that had bound me for so long to my past. I began approaching each challenge with a renewed sense of resilience and determination, refusing to be swayed by the chaos that threatened to overwhelm me.

In the face of uncertainty, I found strength in seeking clarity—**asking tough questions, confronting my fears, and taking decisive action to regain control over my life.** It wasn't an easy journey, but it was necessary to lead me to a place of greater understanding and peace.

Self-reflection on moments of my internal chaos helped me gain clarity amid chaos by identifying the causes of my blindness. By focusing on the moments when I felt most overwhelmed and lost, I could pinpoint the triggers contributing to my sense of chaos and confusion.

Through self-reflection, I am still learning to ask myself difficult questions that help me better understand my emotions, fears, and doubts. This process enabled me to distinguish between external factors beyond my control and internal struggles I could address. By acknowledging and confronting these inner conflicts, I continue untangling the knots of confusion that had bound me to chaos for so long.

I became daring and began delving into my vulnerabilities. This allowed me to gain insights into my thought patterns and beliefs.

Introspection helped me recognize the divine power that gave me the ability to control how to respond to challenging situations, even when external circumstances seemed overwhelming. It has been a game-changer for me.

This self-reflection allowed me to embrace **responsibility for my well-being and peace of mind.** I discovered a newfound inner strength and discernment by seeking clarity amid chaos. This process of introspection and self-discovery empowers you to take decisive action and move toward a life of understanding and peace.

They say **FEAR** can mean two things: Forget Everything and Run, or Face Everything and Rise. The choice is yours. My past reaction was to run, avoid, evade, or dismiss all nearly impossible to conceive or achieve because fear would block the plan of action. The second option of facing it was intimidating, but my faith gave me the confidence to handle the situation with practice. You soon become capable of overcoming any obstacle that comes your way when you know what is necessary and you trust in yourself.

You can employ several things to navigate turbulent waters with grace and resilience:

- Understand your triggers, emotions, and reactions to chaotic situations. Awareness of your internal state can help you respond intentionally rather than impulsively. Without fear and clarity, choose viable solutions.

- Stay focused on the here and now rather than lost in worries about the future or regrets about the past. Mindfulness can help ground you during turbulent times. A Creative Chaos Warrior creates a balance to choose with clarity.

- Build your ability to recognize and manage your emotions effectively. This knowledge will help you understand the feelings of others and navigate interpersonal dynamics with empathy and compassion. Surround yourself with people who uplift and support you. Lean on friends, family, or mentors for guidance, perspective, and emotional support during challenging times.

- Take time to reflect on your values, goals, and priorities. Clarity about your purpose can help you stay focused and resilient when facing chaos and uncertainty. When you see setbacks as temporary obstacles rather than insurmountable barriers, approach adversity with curiosity and resilience.

- Remember, your physical, mental, and emotional well-being is necessary. You are replenishing your energy with exercise, meditation, hobbies, or time in nature. It gives you balance as well.

- Know your limits to protect your time, energy, and resources. Learning to say no helps me to see things that don't align with my priorities. I found a need to prioritize tasks that contribute to my well-being and the goals of my lifestyle.

- I have become open to adapting plans and strategies to dynamic circumstances. Flexibility allows me to swim through unexpected challenges with creativity and resilience while relieving stress.

- Acknowledge and celebrate achievements. This was a foreign concept for me prior. No matter how small the task, I now celebrate. Recognizing your progress and accomplishments will boost your confidence and motivation during challenging times in unique ways.

By incorporating all these strategies into your life, you can cultivate the resilience and grace needed to navigate turbulent waters with strength and poise. It is a goal worth pursuing while you battle confusion and cannot obtain clarity and balance to weigh your options with courage and discernment. I have been blessed beyond imaginable proportions. My friend, you can fight as a Creative Chaos Warrior, too.

In times of chaos and adversity, I now envision facing a beacon of light shining brightly within the encroaching shadows of doubt and fear. I plan to let my inner light radiate during these challenging times; however, it involves several vital affirmations.

I will cultivate a deep sense of self-awareness to understand my emotions, thoughts, and reactions to chaos. By acknowledging and accepting my feelings, I can work through them effectively and prevent them from dimming my light of truth and clarity.

I consciously maintain a more optimistic attitude, focusing on solutions rather than problems. Reframing challenges as chances for growth and lessons, I can keep my inner light burning, even in the darkest moments.

I now prioritize self-care practices that nourish my mind, body, and spirit. Caring for myself physically, emotionally, and mentally can replenish my inner resources and strengthen me to weather the storms of chaos.

I will not hesitate to seek support from friends, family, or professional resources when navigating chaos and adversity. By surrounding myself with a network of positivity and encouragement, I can draw strength from their light to bolster my own.

I now practice mindfulness and grounding techniques to stay present in the moment and connected to my inner light. By anchoring myself in the here and now, I can prevent the chaos from overwhelming me and maintain a sense of calm and clarity. I also rely on faith in God, the ability of spirit, and the perseverance God grants me among the plethora of talents I was unaware I had.

I am nourishing an attitude of gratitude and now focusing on the blessings in my life even amidst the turmoil. By shifting my perspective to see the silver linings and opportunities in adversity, I can keep my inner light aglow with hope and resilience.

By incorporating these strategies into my approach to navigating chaos and adversity, I am creating confidence in my ability to be creative in turmoil, armed with invaluable weapons and faith. God lets the inner light guide me. He shines brightly when you seek Him, guiding you through the darkness, illuminating the path toward a brighter tomorrow, and sharing that with those willing to believe.

In the grand tapestry of your existence, every moment is a creative brushstroke painting the portrait of your life, a masterpiece in progress, which you color with hues of resilience, compassion, and unyielding spirit. Each sunrise whispers promises of new beginnings, urging you to welcome the unknown with open hearts and unwavering courage. Amidst the cacophony of life's symphony, we find solace in the symphony of your inner voice, guiding us through the labyrinth of possibilities and uncertainties. In the crucible of challenges, we forge the steel of our resolve, turning adversity into opportunity and setbacks into stepping stones toward greatness. As we stand at the crossroads of fate and destiny, let us remember that within us lies the power to shape our narrative—to write our own story with wisdom, acts of kindness, and dreams that reach for the stars. With each heartbeat, we breathe life into our aspirations, daring to defy the boundaries of the ordinary and embrace the extraordinary. Let us cherish every moment, triumph, and stumble as a testament to our humanity and capacity to love, heal, and find meaning in the seemingly mundane. As you navigate the labyrinth of existence, let us learn and teach you to walk with purpose and passion, knowing that your journey is a fleeting whisper in the winds of time. However, you will leave a timeless legacy of hope, inspiration, and enduring impact for future generations.

CHAPTER 5

Mastering the Art of Disorder

Are you ready to take on the world? Imagine the thrill of embracing challenges, pushing your limits, and reaching for the stars. Taking risks may seem daunting initially, but it can lead to self-discovery, increased confidence, and expanded horizons. So why not step out of your comfort zone and discover amazing things you may achieve? Why not arm yourself against disorder?

In the thick of chaos, there exists an art that few people dare to master: the art of disorder. As a Creative Chaos Warrior, navigating unpredictability is not just a skill but a way of life. Embracing disorder and uncertainty with open arms, I have gathered insights and tips along my journey to share with fellow warriors seeking to thrive in life's ever-changing landscape.

Mastering the art of disorder as a Creative Chaos Warrior involves adapting to unpredictability and using it to your advantage. These tips will help you deal with information overload and chaotic confusion that can develop with technology.

Conquering the ability to wade through chaos and uncertainty effectively is a valuable skill everyone should possess to decipher the suspense generated from confusion. You can benefit from this in various aspects of your life. Here are some reasons why mastering this art is essential:

- When disorder is present, adaptability allows you to adjust quickly to changing circumstances, making you even better equipped to handle unexpected challenges. You will adapt to acting swiftly. Solving problems will become easier as you conquer uncertainty when chaos is present.

- When creativity is sparked, innovation will take your focus. You will also reveal creativity when you start thinking differently than you did before. It will give you the courage to face disorder confidently. Novel solutions will appear, and your creative mindset will show you alternatives that will gain you clarity.

- Dominating the art of disorder will tune up your problem-solving skills. You can develop an ability to analyze complex situations, identify critical issues, and find practical solutions. You will organize feasible goals instead of a list of insurmountable challenges.

- You will start comprehending how disorder enables you to assess risks effectively. You will make informed decisions even in uncertain situations. You can also seize opportunities while mitigating potential risks promptly.

- Mastering the art of disorder builds resilience by teaching you how to bounce back from obstacles and adversity. You will also learn from failures and setbacks and retain composure under pressure. This ability helps you to develop a constant positive attitude towards challenges. It builds your confidence and authority as you advance in how you respond.

- Encounters with disorders require flexibility and open-mindedness. Governing this art can enhance your ability to adapt and accept change, embrace new ideas, and adjust your plans as needed.

- Disorder challenges you to step out of your routine, confront apprehensions, and discover strengths and capabilities to fend off confusion and inaction. You will become focused on investigating or experimenting with possible solutions.

Mastering the art of disorder is crucial for effective leadership in today's dynamic and unpredictable world. Leaders who can steer around chaos, inspire confidence, guide others through uncertainty, and drive positive outcomes even in challenging situations succeed.

By mastering the art of disorder, you can gain a competitive edge, foster a growth-oriented mindset, and thrive when uncertainty and challenges arise. It's about welcoming chaos as a lesson and testing yourself for growth rather than having a hindrance you can't overcome.

To be a true Creative Chaos Warrior, one must possess the gift of adaptability. When the winds of disorder blow fiercely, the ability to adjust swiftly to shifting circumstances sets you apart. Resilience blooms in the soil of unpredictability, empowering you to overcome feats, emerge stronger, and become bolder with each trial.

Within the chaos lie hidden treasures of creativity waiting to be unleashed. Mastering the art of disorder opens the floodgates of innovation, nudging you to think beyond the conventional boundaries. As a chaos warrior, novelty becomes your ally, paving the way for unconventional solutions and a creative mindset that illuminates the path ahead.

Sharpening your problem-solving skills is paramount in turbulent seas of disorder. By delving deep into the heart of chaos, you can refine your ability to dissect complex situations, unearth critical issues, and craft practical solutions that penetrate the fog of uncertainty.

Assessing risks and seizing opportunities is a priority to handle chaos. In the dance of disorder, perceiving risks and seizing opportunities become second nature to a seasoned creative chaos warrior. By mastering the art of disorder, you acquire the keen insight needed to sail the murky waters confidently, making informed decisions even in the face of ambiguity. The ordeal of chaos tempers your spirit, producing resilience in its wake. As you learn to weather storms and emerge from adversity unscathed, the art of disorder imparts invaluable lessons in bouncing back from setbacks, learning from failures, and standing firm in the face of pressure.

Level-headedness accompanies open-mindedness. They are the twin wings that carry you through the whirlwind of confusion. A precise and level-headed person welcomes new ideas; you expand your horizons and adapt plans with fluidity, adjusting your course as the winds of chaos shift direction.:

Mastering this art of disorder is not merely a quest for survival but a pursuit of personal growth and self-discovery. In the agony of disorder, you confront your fears, discover strengths, and unearth hidden capabilities that empower you to navigate confusion with resolve and action.

In today's dynamic world, leadership can be affected in the face of chaos. Concise leadership requires mastering the art of disorder. Leaders can maneuver their responses through murky seas, inspire confidence, and guide others with clarity through uncertainty, which can become pillars of strength in challenging times.

Care is fundamental to building strong personal, professional, or community relationships. It involves showing empathy, kindness, and consideration for others' emotions and well-being. By demonstrating care, individuals create supportive environments that promote trust, understanding, and mutual respect. It also broadens the ability to resolve confusion in disorder.

Sharing fosters generosity, collaboration, and interconnectedness among people. It encourages exchanging ideas, resources, and experiences, leading to collective growth and unity. By sharing knowledge, skills, and resources, individuals can contribute to the greater good and create a culture of reciprocity and cooperation. Paying it forward becomes conducive to adopting these skills.

Daring to step outside one's comfort zone will lead to personal development, growth, and new opportunities. Taking risks, embracing challenges, and pursuing goals that may seem daunting initially can lead to self-discovery, increased confidence, and expanded horizons. Daring greatly often results in valuable lessons learned and a sense of accomplishment. I can attest to these tips and skill sets being very practical.

Bearing hardships with resilience involves facing adversity with strength, perseverance, and determination. It requires individuals to confront difficult circumstances, setbacks, or obstacles without giving up. By welcoming challenges as lessons for growth, you develop resilience muscle and emerge stronger from trying situations.

Resilience involves adapting to change, managing stress, and returning from setbacks with a positive outlook. Cultivating resilience involves developing coping strategies, seeking support when needed, and maintaining a mindset focused on growth and learning.

CHAPTER 6

Creativity an Unlikely Way to Handle Chaos

When the world around us seems to be in chaos, it's easy to feel overwhelmed and powerless. But what if I told you that embracing creativity in these moments can be the key to unlocking your inner strength and resilience? Yes, you read that right! By unlocking your creativity, you will discover new possibilities and innovative solutions to overcome challenges that life throws your way. At least, that is what is happening to me.

Welcoming innovation will assist you in becoming more adaptable. Creativity is not just about artistry. It is a handy mindset that allows you to think beyond the boundaries of your routine and expand your perspective. It breaks your free routine and limiting beliefs. This gives you ingenuity and an edge in passing through unexpected situations with greater ease.

This creative ability encourages resilience to grow within you. It provides you with an outlet for self-expression and a stress relief outlet. It becomes an emotional platform to help the process. It will help you bounce back from setbacks with incredible grit and focus, as it has helped me. The act of creation can transform the chaos into personal growth and a skill set that will convert the confusion.

This becomes a breeding ground for innovation. It will inspire you to push the limits of conventional thinking and explore new horizons, opening new opportunities for growth and self-discovery. You may uncover hidden talents, personally and professionally, as has occurred with me in uncharted territories.

Implementation of creativity empowers you to reimagine challenges as manageable steps to engage in for personal and professional advancement. It will help you develop a proactive mindset that drives you forward with renewed motivation and purpose. It can make you a published author with a global impact, as it did for me. It has challenged me to become someone entirely foreign yet unique. I embarked on a mission as a Resilience Ambassador to pay forward the transformation it initiated and has continued. Who knew?

Through artistic expression or problem-solving skills, you uncover hidden talents and strengths that deepen your understanding of self. Gifts that God incorporated into your essence. They are meant to be discovered so we can live out our passion authentically, which God has revealed—a torch of truth to what matters in my dictionary of life. You will reveal it when you join the army of warriors.

Your creativity encourages connections with like-minded individuals who share your passion for innovation and self-expression. Collaborating with such individuals offers a sense of camaraderie and unity that bolsters your resilience and encourages your spirit. It made me care more about humanity and value the diversity and similarities of the importance of our mind, body, and soul well-being.

Incorporating creativity during chaos empowers you to transform adversity into opportunity. You develop resilience within uncertainty. So, let your creative flame illuminate the path to resilience. Let innovation flow into your open mind and reach the imagination to create options and solutions. It is phenomenal; you will discover something tailored to your unique character. My voyages through the tumultuous tides of life revealed all that had blocked my reality, the culprits of what caused fear and doubt, all that was limiting my ability to get ahead and feel fulfillment.

After reviewing the unresolved traumas with a new perspective, those trials and tribulations became life lessons. I found the tools that would reveal triggers of insecurity and abandonment were being shown to me. Everything that darkened my joy and vigor was lifted. That whole panorama of what I had missed was loaded with blessings. It was a wow moment for me with God, and my soul was overcome with gratitude. I felt and heard a calling to share my findings with others so that I may cultivate a treasure for their family and future. It was epically incredible and surreal.

Another amazing epiphany I recently discovered is that failure can be an effective teacher, allowing you to develop essential qualities and skills that can shape your character and arm you to battle chaos or adversity. It taught me a treasure trove of knowledge. It helped me recognize the value of perseverance. With it, I found the determination to face those challenges; I was gifted with resilience and specialized in chaos and uncertainty. Additionally, experiencing so many failures nurtured empathy and humility in me. This was all as I was learning to understand and relate to others going through similar struggles.

It also enhances virtues like courage, wisdom, and boldness as you navigate setbacks and start making sounder decisions. You will use failure as a bridge for personal growth and skill development. This will help you build resilience and become a Creative Chaos Warrior, ready to take on any challenge that comes your way. Remember, every failure provides an opportunity to learn and improve. Could you learn to make the most out of chaos and disorder?

As you master the art of becoming a "Creative Chaos Warrior," you will evolve into someone who thrives in chaos and uses it to fuel their creativity. Numerous avenues benefit warriors in their ability and willingness to accept the uncertainty in whatever disorder happens. You will also start letting go of the need for control in your creative process.

Looking at challenges and setbacks as opportunities can fundamentally change how you approach life. You will see each obstacle as a chance to learn, adapt, and improve, especially when you develop resilience that helps you bounce back stronger each time. Your struggles shape your character and provide valuable knowledge to implement in future endeavors.

By acknowledging and learning from past difficulties, you will better handle future storms confidently and gracefully. These experiences are a foundation for developing problem-solving skills, emotional intelligence, and greater self-awareness. Every stumble and fall is a stepping stone towards personal growth and empowerment.

So, when facing challenges and chaos in life, remember that your past experiences have equipped you with the strength and wisdom needed to navigate through them. Trust in your ability to overcome obstacles, embrace the journey of growth, and continue forging ahead with resilience and determination, arming yourself into a living example of a warrior who can battle through obstacles that prevent you from pursuing your purpose.

Going into the unknown was a very transformative experience for me, and it can also be for you. It opens new possibilities and sparks fresh ideas. When you venture outside your familiar territory, you must think differently, adapt quickly, and approach problems from new angles. Shifting your perspective can lead to innovative solutions and creative breakthroughs you may not have thought conceivable. Moving into uncharted territory pushes you to think beyond conventional boundaries and explore unconventional approaches.

You encounter new people, ideas, and perspectives by exposing yourself to unfamiliar situations. These new connections can inspire you, challenge your assumptions, and lead you to novel insights you wouldn't have encountered otherwise. When faced with the unknown, you must adapt quickly and think independently. This adaptive mindset encourages flexibility, resourcefulness, and the ability to find innovative solutions to unexpected challenges.

These strategies provide valuable insights that give you well-informed decisions and a guide to adjust your creative arsenal. Continuous learning and improvement will increase your personal growth. It will encourage experimentation, embrace failures as learning opportunities, and stay adaptable to change. You will find more ways to resolve instead of excuses to avoid the situation.

Embrace the power of chaos to fuel your creative pursuits. Let it catalyze innovation, propelling you towards breakthrough moments in your artistic journey. Transform chaotic energy into a force for productive creativity, channeling the unpredictable into inspired work.

In conclusion, remember that chaos is not your enemy—it's a gateway to transformation. It is a fountain of courage, curiosity, and open-mindedness of a Creative Chaos Warrior who embraces the unknown, confronts challenges head-on, and witnesses the magic that unfolds when chaos and creativity collide. Face adversity with a newfound purpose, using it as a springboard to reach new heights in your work and life.

Becoming a Creative Chaos Warrior makes you focused on adopting the unpredictable nature of confusion, which, at times, can be overwhelming. I learned this when handling aspects of the creative process, and it can be especially true if you have yet to gain experience applying it. But just as an artist mixes his palette to apply the shades and tones he prefers, so can you. **Experiment and investigate** what works well for you. You can use your authenticity here. The technique, the tools, and your approach will be more precise as you find the order in that creative chaos. You will see beauty and resilience as you develop your style. The point is it may look chaotic to start, but the tapestry of resilience will evolve from the mess. You can create a masterpiece of your life even if it seems impossible.

Adapting creative strategies in response to new information is crucial for staying innovative and relevant. Once you develop an **agile mindset**, you can quickly change based on the situation. You will break down your plan into smaller, manageable tasks which can be modified. Brainstorming sessions will be second nature and help you generate new ideas and solutions. You will build flexibility into your creative process by allowing room for experimentation and exploration. You will avoid rigid structures hindering your ability to pivot and adapt to new information. You will anticipate different scenarios and develop plans for potential changes. By preparing for various outcomes, you can respond more effectively to unexpected developments and adjust your creative strategies accordingly. You will feel fortified with knowledge you would have never discovered if you had let fear and unpredictability throw you off.

I aim to inspire you to see chaos not as a hindrance but as a source of creative potential that can lead to transformative outcomes in your work and life, as it has for me. Once you've eliminated a dome of your limitations from your emotional luggage, your vision will be more apparent. You'll be able to confront and eliminate the potential problems or catastrophes that once paralyzed you helpless. Solutions and resources eliminate the patterns that repeatedly blocked your progress in the past. You can now be liberated for growth, believing in yourself, and gaining internal peace to pursue your dreams, passion, purpose, and mission.

Now, imagine yourself in a world where challenges are no longer insurmountable obstacles but rather as exciting opportunities for growth and learning! The possibilities are endless when we shift our perspective and approach challenges with enthusiasm and a willingness to learn. Get ready to embrace the thrill of overcoming obstacles and unlocking your full potential!

CHAPTER 7

Embracing Acceptance Amidst Turbulence

Acceptance is a formidable force in the face of chaos. It has been my guiding light through the darkest of storms. Its power transcends mere resignation, offering a path to inner peace and resilience through life's trials and tribulations. This journey of acceptance has been deeply personal, marked by many challenges that tested my very essence, rattling my emotional intelligence until I found how liberating it is to face fears and unresolved emotions.

At the tender age of seven, I was branded a mistake, a label that etched itself into the depths of my being. The sting of those words lingered, shaping my perception of self-worth and belonging. Yet, through the crucible of acceptance, the sting of those words lingered, shaping my perception of self-worth and belonging. Yet, through the crucible of acceptance, I found the courage to embrace my uniqueness, turning perceived flaws into strengths. I became bold and daring, learning the path of least resistance and weighing the viable options to combat chaos.

Wheelchair-bound, my muscles atrophied, rendering the simplest of tasks monumental feats. The inability to conceive children further compounded my sense of inadequacy, shattering dreams of motherhood. But within the confines of my wheelchair, I discovered a resilience that defied limitations. A strength was born of acceptance and perseverance.

Numerous surgeries punctuated my journey, each leaving its mark. It became a testament to the fragility of the human body. Yet, with each scar came a deeper appreciation for life's fragility and resilience. Through acceptance, I learned to navigate the uncertainty of my health journey with grace and determination, refusing to let setbacks define me.

Loss became a familiar companion regarding jobs, relationships, or homes, slipping through my fingers like grains of sand. Yet, during the upheaval, acceptance offered solace. It became a reminder that endings are often beginnings in disguise. Being bilingual and versatile allowed me to embrace change as an opportunity for growth, weaving the tapestry of my life with threads of resilience and adaptability.

The journey of acceptance is fraught with challenges, yet the promise of transformation lies within its crucible. Through self-reflection and empathy, I forged more profound connections with myself and others, fostering a sense of community. I discovered a shared purpose. Embracing acceptance became a beacon of hope amidst my life's chaos.

Acceptance is not merely a passive surrender to fate but a powerful tool for self-discovery and growth. By embracing acceptance, you cultivate resilience, adaptability, and a proactive approach to navigating uncertainties. When you harness the power of acceptance and embark on a transformation journey, the indomitable spirit of the human heart illuminates the journey.

Acceptance is about acknowledging the hand we've been dealt and finding strength and resilience in the face of adversity. It's about turning your scars into badges of honor and your struggles into stepping stones toward growth. Through acceptance, you can find peace where chaos happens. You build courage amidst uncertainty. It is a journey that requires you to build courage, humility, and firm faith in the inherent goodness of life.

By embracing acceptance, you open yourself up to a world of possibilities. It has become a world where setbacks are not roadblocks but mere detours, leading you to new destinations. This journey requires you to relinquish your attachments and expectations and trust God's wisdom. You are surrendering to the flow of life; you can navigate its turbulent waters with grace and resilience.

You need to confront your deepest fears and insecurities to gain acceptance. It is a journey that requires us to let go of the need for control and surrender to the unknown with faith and courage. Through acceptance, you can find strength in your weaknesses and beauty in your imperfections. This journey requires you to let go of the past and face the present with gratitude and humility.

By embracing acceptance, you can find peace in chaos and strength in uncertainty. This journey requires trust in the inherent goodness of life and belief in the power of resilience and hope. Through acceptance, you will find meaning in your struggles and purpose in your pain. It requires you to "Let go and let in God" and embrace the beauty of life's unpredictability.

You can find freedom by overcoming the chaos and joy amidst the sorrow. This journey requires you to release your need for control and surrender to life's flow with open hearts and minds. Through acceptance, you find peace in the storm and light in the darkness.

It requires you to embrace the fullness of life, with all its joys and sorrows, and trust in God's wisdom.

Acceptance reminds me that endings are often beginnings in disguise and that something more significant is coming than those plans that ended unexpectedly. Being bilingual made me versatile. I now embrace change as an opportunity for growth. It is a great foundation for being grateful for and appreciating all the beneficial knowledge it has given me.

Acceptance is not merely a passive surrender to fate, but a powerful tool for self-discovery and growth. By embracing acceptance, we cultivate **adaptability, flexibility, and a proactive approach** to navigating life's uncertainties. When we harness the power of acceptance and embark on a journey of transformation illuminated by the indomitable spirit of the human heart, we cultivate adaptability, flexibility, and a proactive approach to navigating life's uncertainties.

The potency of acceptance is a formidable force against the chaos that permeates our lives. It has metamorphosed from a mere concept into a transformative tool, altering my perceptions and interactions with life's unpredictable forces. Acceptance, far from being a passive surrender to chaos, is a **deliberate choice**—an acknowledgment of reality unclouded by youthful misconceptions. This newfound understanding lacks resistance, freeing me from fear and denial. I confront turmoil without trepidation, viewing it as a challenge to be embraced, a path to growth previously unexplored. Indeed, to dismiss acceptance is to deprive oneself of the wisdom it bestows.

Acceptance is the gateway to **inner peace and strength** previously untapped when confronted with adversity or unforeseen circumstances. No longer do I succumb to fear and anxiety; rather, I embrace the present moment with open arms, trusting in the wisdom of a higher power. Acceptance of life's impermanence has endowed me with the resilience to navigate turbulent waters with grace and determination. Where frustration once reigned, now resides a steadfast resolve to seek solutions—a monumental shift that proves invaluable when chaos descends.

Embracing acceptance is a continuous practice, an ongoing dare to summon courage and humility. It beckons one to relinquish attachments and expectations, surrendering to the flow of life with newfound ease. In doing so, a taste of inner freedom and empowerment is savored, permeating every facet of existence. Through acceptance, trust in the innate order of life blossoms despite the chaos that plagues us.

Ultimately, acceptance has been my liberation, a tangible release from the grip of resistance, ushering peace into the depths of my being. By embracing life's ebbs and flows, I have unearthed a profound sense of presence and purpose.

Within the tumultuous realm of chaos and uncertainty, acceptance is a beacon of resilience and inner strength—a bulwark against the relentless waves of unpredictability. Through its embrace, one learns to navigate challenges with poise and determination, transcending adversity with unwavering resolve. Let us delve deeper into this concept, illuminated by personal examples.

In the face of profound loss, such as the passing of my father, acceptance enabled me to confront and process my emotions without denial. By acknowledging the inevitability of loss, I traversed the stages of grief with newfound ease, finding solace in cherished memories and enduring love. Similarly, amidst career instability, acceptance allowed me to confront uncertainties with resilience rather than succumbing to anxiety. Instead of considering setbacks and failures, I embrace them as opportunities for growth and self-discovery.

Relationships, too, are fraught with trials and tribulations. Acceptance in this context involves acknowledging differences and conflicts, fostering better communication, and understanding each other. By choosing acceptance over resignation, healthier and more meaningful relationships are forged. After forty-one years of living trials and tribulations, I tested this theory in my marriage.

Even in the face of health challenges, acceptance is a source of courage and resilience. By confronting illness openly and seeking support, one can navigate one's health journey with determination and hope. Focusing on what you control empowers you to take responsibility for your well-being, fostering a sense of a resilient lifestyle.

Amidst widespread uncertainty and the global pandemic, acceptance proved vital in maintaining mental stability. By embracing acceptance, one can adapt to new norms and find ways to stay connected.

Acceptance, however, extends beyond personal growth—it is a catalyst for societal change. By sharing our stories of resilience and transformation, we inspire others to embrace acceptance as a tool for development and self-discovery. Through self-reflection and empathy, we foster a sense of community and shared purpose.

In conclusion, embracing acceptance is not a surrender to weakness but a wellspring of grit and optimism amidst life's turbulent seas. By embracing acceptance, you foster resilience, flexibility, and a forward-looking mindset in confronting the unknown. So, let's seize the transformative power of acceptance and embark on an exploration of self-discovery.

CHAPTER 8

Did You Know You Can Become a Designer?

Imagine a world where you hold the power to design a life that reflects your deepest aspirations. This world is not a distant dream; it's within your reach. Welcome to the journey of unlocking your innate designer, where the canvas of your life awaits the vibrant strokes of your imagination.

Together, we'll uncover the secrets of becoming a Creative Chaos Warrior—a fearless designer ready to conquer adversity, confusion, and disorder. By embracing the transformative might of creativity, you'll learn to navigate life's complexities with purpose and passion, as I did.

Unlocking the innate designer within you can open an undiscovered world of creativity and innovation. Picture an impact waiting to be unleashed, especially when overcoming uncertainty. Designing is a way of thinking, problem-solving, and communicating ideas. I did not know that igniting a passion for design and unlocking creative potential would come in handy in my life, and nothing pleases me more than to share it with you.

I am actively becoming a Creative Chaos Warrior, and things are very different. I can now battle adversity, confusion, and disorder that previously blocked my path and purpose. I want you to experience this as well, and not only that, but pass it on to those around you. Cultivating a deep passion for creativity is essential in unleashing the designer within you.

Just as designers have a unique ability to blend artistry with functionality, you can start creating solutions that look appealing and serve a purpose. Approaching problems from multiple perspectives and welcoming complex challenges are chances you can be your designer. One that creates meaningful and impactful designs that address needs while conveying a compelling message or story. A resilient foundation of problem-solving skills is at the core of being a designer. Designers thrive on tackling challenges and finding innovative solutions in a mess. Guess what? You can, too. How can that be? You may ask. By honing skills and developing your unique design style, you create a lasting impact on society and culture.

One of the most exciting aspects of becoming this designer is the versatility and adaptability you obtain. With the opportunity to work across various mediums and disciplines, you find a diverse and dynamic approach. You are exploring different areas that help you uncover hidden talents—discovering new interests that expand your creative horizons. Considering it helped me battle fear, lack of self-confidence, and the inability to find a way out of chaos.

Think about it: design shapes our interactions with the world around us. It enhances daily experiences. It influences perceptions, behaviors, and emotions. Through your creations, you are leaving a lasting impact on this world. I began to welcome a lifelong hunger for learning, always curious and open-minded. Long ago. Secretly, it contributed to the collective design of my life's tapestry. A design is constantly evolving, and I was not conscious of this. Being driven by advancements and preferences will undoubtedly change your views.

With your unique creativity, you can envision a successful and fulfilling life. Sometimes, when you get busy with yourself, you discover amazing secrets of a hidden past that you were oblivious to. Somewhere along my epic transformation, a fog of traumas and unresolved emotions from a long-forgotten past had formed. After deep introspection, I began obtaining clarity on past events I had assumed were unapproachable or had no solutions.

I did not know the destiny waiting to be explored and unraveled would be an unbelievable miracle. With a mixture of trepidation and excitement coursing through me, I made my way to where I find myself today: a completely different mindset, a rejuvenated soul, and a massive dose of faith. I am so grateful for discovering a wealth of knowledge I had not seen nor ever applied before. Stepping through that uncomfortable zone rewarded me with victorious battles. I acquired valuable tools and tips to wade through the bombardment of information overload that exists today.

That mass of half-truths in me created a fog of confusion, a cloud of uncertainty that evolved into fear or apprehension. It is challenging to handle when you do not know how to confront a battle. You become petrified by fear, clueless, vulnerable, and helpless. But thanks to life's lessons, I finally read and educated myself on what would transform me into a Creative Chaos Warrior. This is worth sharing with those who suffer and see a way to transcend the chaos and teach others the same.

I finally heard God's message. Somehow, I feel I have been chosen for a journey with a purpose far more significant than I dreamed. However, that would test my courage, unravel the mysteries of my past, and shape my future. A legacy I would love to leave behind for others to share. Are you prepared to embark on this enigmatic adventure with me? Are you ready to get busy with what you can control? To find logical resolutions and create a stable source of valuable wisdom in life?

With all this breakthrough, my heart softened, and forgiveness opened opportunities. Chances to become creative, expand, and awaken the artist dormant in me for so long. With deep breaths and total commitment, I was committed to pulling the real Martie Smith out. God was getting me ready to embrace everything with more clarity. And open the canvas that could document how I became a warrior of chaos that once ignited trauma and hardship in me for so many years. This has taught me ways to overcome, surpass, and transcend.

Recalling my ripe age of eighteen, I was drawn into a whirlwind of events that would forever change my life. That was where the formative process ensuing in my backdrop began. God orchestrated combat plans and logistics for me to be armored with faith, confidence, courage, and perseverance. It is a spiritual war, with basic training and mini battles to teach me strategies and plan Bs to bounce back and respond without falling apart.

I always wanted to express myself. I had a scholarship in art but needed help to get my parent's approval to accept it. I rebelled and quit drawing and painting, burying that talent. My creativity went dormant for decades until I stumbled on another avenue of creativity. The aptitude to and dare to create them and dream. The possibility to transform chaos into creativity. I know to arm myself with creativity and share my story to leave a legacy of hope and resilience. All those were waiting to be implemented and not to face a trail of useless battles with no resolve. How can l become creative?

This defining moment began with realizing that all that prevented me from progressing was my own doing and everything to do with my lack of knowledge. In that aha moment, I could now see how things always played out a mess and how I battled my insecurity with no tools. It showed me how my responses were reactive instead of well-thought-out plans for viable solutions to overcome the disarray. I constantly faced it.

Back then, I just knew l wanted to eliminate the idea of having to choose. I had convinced myself that I couldn't make a good decision. Boy, was I wrong there? My indecisiveness left an aftermath of chaos in my brain. That would inevitably form the emotional battlefield I constantly entered. But I had no clue l was the culprit. I always found myself pending to go to war. I had no idea what tools or weapons to handle the chaos. All that turned into a catastrophic mumble jumble in my limited mind.

The enemy was my lack of love and consciousness. This kept this future warrior at bay, never advancing to overcome obstacles and have clarity. Thanks to God and my introspection reviewing my past decisions, it showed a constant obstacle for me; I couldn't see my responsibility as the main factor. I had learned to defend myself by blaming everything and everyone around me. But I needed to open my eyes and see the whole panorama of my life.

Controlling my destiny by crafting my story kindled a fire within my soul. With newfound determination, I embarked on my journey of self-discovery, ready to embrace the unknown and unlock my hidden potential. I was always driven but seemed to go every which way, but I was loose and needed a destination in sight.

The path ahead was shrouded in mystery, but curiosity helped me face it with unwavering courage and a sense of purpose.

I sensed that the road to becoming the master designer of my life would be filled with challenges and uncertainties, but I felt determined to overcome them all. I had a beacon of love and light with me. It was God showing me the plans instead of me flying by the seat of my pants. His timing is perfect.

I felt renewed empowerment and liberation with each step I took. The canvas of my life was being fabricated before me, blank and waiting to be adorned with the vibrant colors of my imagination. As I dared to delve deeper into the realm of creativity and self-expression, I uncovered layers of myself that had long been dormant, waiting to be awakened.

Every choice now made, every brushstroke applied, reflecting my innermost desires and aspirations. The journey is not easy, but the rewards would be worthwhile. Each day, I grow more confident in my abilities and more attuned to my heart and soul rhythm. This Creative Chaos Warrior went on a quest to unlock creativity, embrace the power of design, and shape a life that was indeed unique. The future is uncertain, but I face it with fierce determination and faith in the beauty of my dreams and all the blessings granted.

Imagine the thrill of chasing your dreams and purpose with all your heart! When your passion and purpose align, it sets the stage for an unstoppable force that propels you toward your goals. So, buckle up, enjoy the ride, and confidently embrace the journey because you're headed towards greatness!

When you get brutally honest and start admitting you don't know, you realize you don't know. I recognized that my GPA was excellent, yet I knew I didn't know much about living life. I was gathering materials to create, but I never unpacked them to start painting the canvas of my life with accurate strokes of authenticity. What an incredible discovery it was.

Think about it - your creator designed the blueprint of your life, but it's up to you to transform it into a masterpiece. Your decisions today will shape your destiny tomorrow, so why not take charge and become the ultimate designer of your life? So, are you ready to unleash your creativity and design a life you've always wanted? Have you ever wondered how to unlock your creativity and become a master designer of your life? The possibilities are endless, and discovering your true potential is humbling and amazing. It all starts with making honest choices and unpacking the materials you've been gathering to paint the canvas of your life with strokes of authenticity.

CHAPTER 9

From Chaos to Clarity, the Journey Continues

This book, Creative Chaos Warrior, explores overcoming fear and doubt through faith, introspection, and resilience. In the face of challenges, I often found myself engulfed in turmoil. Back then, I strayed from truths, becoming distracted by the dazzling illusions of the world. These distractions would usually lead me to a downward spiral that felt uncontrollable, akin to approaching an entrance to Hell.

For me, chaos represented hell, which I once believed was an inevitable part of life. I felt I had to endure it alone, unaware that it stemmed from a lack of discipline, allowing disorder to take over. Upon further reflection, I realized that confusion breeds anxiety. Fear begets insecurity and doubt. This was a toxic cycle that left me feeling paralyzed and trapped in a turmoil of self-doubt and harsh self-judgment.

Recognizing the need for change, I confronted my fears and doubts with the light of truth and faith. By rebuilding my foundation on principles of self-control and order, I set out to banish some of those shadows of chaos and confusion. Embracing my insecurities and anxieties, I later discovered strength in resilience and courage.

Each step forward was a means to chip away at the walls of depression and dread, paving the way for a renewed sense of purpose and vitality in my spirit. This journey taught me to rise above darkness, empowered by a commitment to personal growth and truth, and armored with my faith in God to protect me from enticing distractions that would make me weak and want to give up.

Now, I am fully armed with determination and guided by values of authenticity and integrity. I continuously evolve and navigate challenges with compassion, kindness, and empathy. By binding myself to others in unity and concern for harmony in this world, I now spread hope and embrace obstacles as opportunities for growth and learning. You can learn all these things, too, my friend. It simply takes practice and attention to the present moment.

May you learn to hold onto the flame of hope, lighting the path toward a future brimming with promise and purpose. Stand tall in uncertainty, drawing courage from within your heart. Together, with untiring resolve and collective strength, you can overcome many obstacles, emerge triumphant, and resist turmoil's grip, just like I have.

The following questions always haunted me, but now, with the passing years, I can dismiss them. They may resonate with you: What in the world did I do to deserve this? Did you ever ask yourself that question? Did you ever wonder what you did to imagine a life like you have or what caused it to be in your situation?

Well, nothing happens by accident, and there are no coincidences. It's just part of the grand tapestry of existence. You don't want to be a victim, but sometimes you unknowingly make yourself one.

With that process, you tend to cause chaos—unwanted chaos—on top of the chaos that's already happening in the world all around. No one gets away from it; the only difference is how you choose to respond to it.

You choose what path to take when faced with confusion and chaos. Those choices lead to consequences, be they negative or positive. Now, I invite you to embark with me on this adventure, a journey that has spanned over six decades of my life. My journey has taught me to navigate through the chaos, to arm myself with the protection, resilience, and strength needed to rise from the ashes—to become a warrior always ready to face life's challenges head-on, without fear.

First and foremost, the most critical step is to sort through the mess. You must learn to separate what is a part of you, what doesn't serve you, and what hinders your growth. Doing so creates space for clarity in your life, clearing out the clutter that obscures your true path forward.

Reflecting on my life, I recall profound chaos and confusion. The days when it felt like the world was collapsing around me, suffocating me with its weight. During those times, I realized the importance of resilience - of arming myself with the strength to weather life's storms. I somehow innately got through many tribulations. But now, I see it was my God-given ability to be resilient—an ability instilled deeply in all. We just don't know. We carry it deep in our souls.

One memory stands out vividly in my mind. During the Pandemic, I stood at a crossroads, unsure which path to take. The chaos within me mirrored the howling winds outside, threatening to consume me. At that moment, I chose to confront the chaos head-on, embrace the uncertainty, and transform it into an opportunity for growth. I decided to be the change instead of waiting for things to change.

Sorting through my emotions, thoughts, and fears, I began to discern what was essential to my being. I wanted subconsciously to let go of the baggage weighing me down. The self-doubt and insecurities that held me back were being identified with introspection. In doing so, I could create space for clarity to emerge, for a sense of purpose to guide me forward. I did not know that back then, it would take me down many dead-end paths, nor that it would change my lifestyle.

As you navigate through the maze of chaos and confusion, it is essential to maintain a sense of transparency and purpose. By shedding light on your innermost desires and motivations, you can begin to unravel the tangled webs of uncertainty that cloud your judgment and hinder your progress.

It is easy to succumb to feelings of helplessness and despair in the face of adversity. However, true warriors learn to rise above the chaos, finding strength amid turmoil and courage in the face of uncertainty. It is during these challenging moments that your true character is revealed, and your innate resilience is put to the test.

I embraced my journey ahead with an open heart and a steadfast mind. Trusting in overcoming whatever obstacles came my way through adversity, I grew and evolved. Remember, you are not alone on this path; others have walked before you and will stand beside you as you face the trials ahead.

So, take a deep breath, learn to steel yourself against the storm, and march forward with unwavering determination. The road ahead may be tense with challenges, but remember, it is during the chaos that a true warrior emerges and thrives. Are you ready to embrace the unknown and discover the strength within you?

Going into the depths of chaos, with uncertainty lurking around every corner makes it easy to lose sight of our true purpose. But within the noise and tumult lies your opportunity for transformation, a chance to emerge from the shadows stronger and more resilient than ever. I am living proof of this process and invite you to consider learning to adapt skills that will keep you from falling apart.

As you ride through the twists and turns along your journey, remember that clarity is not always found in the absence of chaos but in how you choose to navigate it. The challenges that come your way are occasions for growth and self-discovery. Believe in your capability to overcome whatever obstacles stand in your path and emerge victorious on the other side. Have faith. It builds an armor of hope.

The journey of a warrior is challenging, but it is a path worth traveling. With each step you take and each obstacle you overcome, you get closer to unlocking your true potential and realizing your ultimate destiny. So, stand tall, face the chaos head-on, and embrace the warrior within you. Your journey awaits, and the world is yours to conquer. Creating clarity is not a one-time task but an ongoing process—a continuous effort to sift through the noise of daily life and focus on what truly matters. It requires honesty with oneself, a willingness to confront the shadows within you, and embrace the light that shines through.

As I navigate the chaos, my thoughts, actions, aspirations, and core values become apparent. I am forging a path that resonates with my most profound truths. Clarity has brought me a sense of liberation—a newfound freedom to pursue passions, chase dreams, and conquer my fears. It empowers me to stand tall in the face of adversity to weather life's storms with grace and resilience.

In creating clarity, I am discovering the power of intention—consciously choosing my responses to life's challenges. Instead of being swept away by the currents of chaos, I am learning to anchor myself in the present moment and respond with mindfulness and wisdom.

The journey from chaos to clarity is challenging and linear. It is a winding path filled with twists and turns, setbacks, and triumphs. It demands you to possess courage, perseverance, and a willingness to embrace the unknown.

Yet, with each step taken and each obstacle overcome, I grow more vital, resilient, and attuned to the whispers of my soul. This clarity is not a destination but a way of being—a state of mind that allows you to navigate the complexities of life with grace and purpose. It is conscious of all that you live.

So, my dear reader, I invite you to embark on your journey from chaos to clarity. Arm yourself with the strength of a warrior and obtain the resilience of a phoenix rising from the embers. Embrace the chaos, confront the confusion, and carve out a path leading you to inner peace and fulfillment.

Remember, the journey may be with extended family, and the road may be rough, but clarity will increase. It will move you closer to the truth residing within you. Trust yourself, the process, and the transformative power of embracing chaos and finding clarity. This fundamental skill can significantly enhance one's ability to thrive in chaotic situations. You will notice that you are surviving challenging circumstances and emerging stronger and more resilient.

Clarity allows you to comprehend complexity and ambiguity without losing sight of your goals and values. It is about finding balance amid disorder, maintaining a sense of purpose, and direction even when the path ahead seems uncertain. By setting clear intentions, establishing priorities, and staying true to one's vision, you can anchor down in a sea of chaos and steer your course with confidence and determination.

Ultimately, learning to traverse chaos with clarity is a journey—a continuous process of growth, learning, and self-discovery. It requires your willingness to embrace discomfort and uncertainty. But the rewards are tremendous: leaving a more profound sense of purpose, a robust capacity for resilience, and a deeper connection to oneself loaded with wisdom.

So, dear reader, I invite you to embark on this courageous journey—to step boldly into the chaos, armed with clarity and determination, and discover the transformative power within you. Embrace the fear, seek the lessons, and trust in your ability to navigate the chaos with grace and wisdom. May you find clarity during your confusion, strength in facing adversity, and inspiration in the heart of chaos.

CHAPTER 10

An Unlikely Warrior is Born

Would becoming a Creative Chaos Warrior be a possibility? Within you lies a hidden warrior, ready to fight for something. Perhaps you have a burning desire to find a transformation like I managed. That would make you rise with enthusiasm and gusto for life—obtaining an arsenal of courage that drives you with determination—possessing a beaming warmth and gratitude for others. An overflowing heart overflows with compassion. A source of power in your spirit that becomes unbreakable, that forges strength in your will. A foundation that gives you grace to face challenges with courage. Vitamins that allow you to face adversity with courage and stand firm on your principles with honor.

You become the hero of your story; you discover the light in the darkness. Enlisting yourself on a mission to become an example to follow is achievable. We can rebuild the fibers of family and community together. That will allow us each an opportunity to grow, share, and thrive with our different talents and treasures.

My newly claimed courage, self-compassion, and unwavering faith in God fueled a transformative path. In the face of past adversity, I find healing and growth through reflection and self-care practices. My resilience shines through as I learn to confront my inner demons with courage, compassion, and a willingness to transform my pain into strength. All this with a suitable dosage of faith in God, who has armed me as a warrior.

The shadows of my past challenges and the echoes of pain that once defined me No longer haunt me with doubt. The uncertainty is diffusing now, and I choose a path that illuminates me with healing and personal growth. A transformative power that unearthed strength within me that had long been buried under layers of hurt I was trying to protect myself from. The change had to initiate with me. I had to assume the responsibility of learning. It was deciphering the roadmap and plan of attack to combat chaos effectively. So, the clarity would remain sharp, and I had to hone skills I was discovering with a creative mindset accentuating the positive. This would clear a path to finding solutions to questions that visited me regularly.

With each step forward, my resilience emerged as a beacon, guiding me through the darkest corners of my soul. The swamp of confusion and irrelevancy I had created and swam in constantly has been drained. I confronted my inner demons not with fear but with firm courage and a sense of compassion that embraced the wounded parts of myself.

As I walked this path of self-discovery and redemption, I found solace in surrendering to a force greater than myself. It was God. With a heart full of faith, I realized I was not alone in this battle; I was armed as a warrior with divine grace and guidance. I confronted my inner demons not with fear but with unwavering courage and a sense of compassion that embraced the wounded parts of myself.

As I walked this path of self-discovery and redemption, I found solace in surrendering to a force greater than me. I let go and let God. With a heart full of faith in Him, I realized that I was not alone in this battle; I was being armed as a warrior with divine grace and guidance—the guidance I have sought since childhood.

When faced with unexpected changes in life, such as relocation, 49 moves, relationship endings engaged twice, the third time was a charm. With health issues, twenty-six surgeries for me, and a debilitating condition, I could adapt with grace and resilience. It taught me to approach each new chapter with an open mind, seeing change as an opportunity for evolution, self-discovery, and new purpose.

Improving my health and adopting fitness also was a catalyst. At sixty-two, I became a personal trainer and made healthy eating habits a lifestyle. Despite my mobility struggles and moments of doubt, I persevered with courage and determination, celebrating each small victory. I transformed my body, losing seventy pounds and seventy inches. I lost weight but gained so many more things I never thought possible.

All these taught me to celebrate each small victory along the way, inspiring me to find more. When you practice gratitude during adversity, you start focusing on the positive aspects of life. You acknowledge the blessings, small joys, and moments of kindness around you. With that, you cultivate a sense of appreciation that powers resilience and strengthens your emotional well-being. It helps you battle confusion and chaos, keeping you focused with clarity and certainty.

I also learned that by volunteering for a cause close to my heart, I could dedicate my time and energy to positively impacting my community. My enthusiasm and gratitude helped me perceive hope. If you work tirelessly to support others, creativity is born.

I even decided to pursue further education. I want to learn new skills despite feeling intimidated by the challenges ahead. With a passionate desire for personal growth and development, I could approach my studies with enthusiasm and determination. Embracing the journey with open arms, knowledge became my friend, which I relied on when I didn't have friends. When I returned to school and acquired a degree from medical school as a Radiation Therapist, treating cancer patients, it taught me how to live. Who knew then, that death and dying would teach me about living and thriving?

That is when resilience began augmenting my life more. I was wheelchair-dependent and had to abandon my career. I faced setbacks, and yes, job loss and rejection were traumatic, but I refused to give up. With determination and more faith, I actively found new opportunities while trying to navigate my career options. Once all those tools were utilized, I gained knowledge and wisdom. Strengths and weaknesses were seen vividly. I was commencing building the confidence to share my story.

That is when I began launching my way out of any familiar routine. I found myself uncomfortable, yet I decided to write and speak about my ability to solve impossibilities. I discovered a creative artist who could shut the door on disillusions. When I started writing and publicly speaking, my creative expression was tuned into sharing and caring. That lamp lit up my passion.

Sharing your resilience and personal transformation journey with others is also cathartic. It makes you vulnerable, empathetic, and more user-friendly with compassionate fervor by vulnerably sharing challenges, triumphs, and lessons learned. Lots of great things begin happening.

You begin deciphering who you are. What makes you thrive? What are your limitations? You reveal patterns of what has held you back and discover a library of options. You grow an appetite for knowledge—a desire to build a character based on authenticity. You develop integrity, honor, and trustworthiness. And the best part is when you start craving this bounce-back ability for others to feel that joy of life. You become the kind of person who inspires and empowers those around you.

Those warriors find their inner strength and live with passion and purpose. You learn that battling adversity and trailblazing with creativity can form a legacy of hope and combatting things that cause mayhem.

That sense of inner strength, positivity, and empowerment enables you to navigate life's challenges flexibly. I have nurtured a deep-rooted sense of self-love, which has sustained me through life's tides. My journey toward healing has taught me the value of vulnerability and authenticity, allowing me to connect with others profoundly and share my story with courage and compassion.

I carry with me the wisdom of my experiences and the resilience of my spirit. I am no longer defined by a chaotic past but by the strength that emerges from it. In the face of adversity, I stand tall with hope and inspiration. I am becoming a living testament to the power of healing, growth, and transformation. My journey showed me the human spirit, capable of rising from the depths of despair to soar to new heights of empowerment and fulfillment.

With each passing day, I walk with grace, guided by the light illuminating and walking my path and inspiring others to embark on their journey of healing and transformation.

I now leave you with tools and weapons to become a warrior for light, a symbol of resilience, and a living embodiment of the transformative power of the human spirit. Your story can also testify to the infinite possibilities that await you. I dare you to embark on the journey of self-discovery and healing. I promise it will amaze you.

My emphasis is now on love (God) and kindness, constantly reminding me of the importance of nurturing meaningful connections with others. You grow by reaching out to friends, family, and community members. In acts of service and fostering

genuine bonds, you create a supportive network that uplifts each other during joyful and challenging moments. By clarifying your values, envisioning aspirations, and taking deliberate steps toward objectives, you locate the bearings of your life that lead to greater fulfillment and self-discovery.

My journey underscores the significance of well-being and a lifestyle that helps with life's challenges. The most rewarding part of delivering my message of hope and inspiration is that it serves as a beacon for those facing their struggles. By sharing your story, you offer support and encouragement, becoming a source of positivity and resilience for those around you. Surprisingly, as I have found out, you will create a ripple effect with a transformation within communities and beyond frontiers to a global level to become more flexible and prepared for chaos.

Incorporating all these principles into your life can help embody the spirit of hope, resilience, and compassion. This process has taken over my soul, inspiring positive change within others and the world. So, my friend, consider my tips to build your armor of goodness and thy shield of hope. Becoming a warrior in the battle for goodness, justice, and love in chaos built my resilience.

I discovered that in me lies an unlikely warrior, armed and ready to fight for what is correct, sound, and just—to fight for what matters, to fight what clouds vision. Arm yourself with hope, resilience, and faith. Train in the things that keep you grounded and focused. Rise courageously, with determination in your eyes, and be ready to share your heart full of compassion with humanity.

May your spirit always be unbreakable, your will immovable, and your determination unshaken. May you be ready to face challenges with courage, embrace adversity with strength, and stand up for your principles with honor.

May you learn to be a hero of your story, spread the light in the world's darkness, and be the example to follow for a better future. Let thy sword become truth; thy armor be loaded with creativity and goodness; thy shield is hope and resilience in the battle for goodness, justice, and love. Become a Creative Chaos Warrior, my friend. It will transform your life. Get prepared for the new you. Start your army of warriors, and let's transform humanity.

CHAPTER 11

Turning Life's Chaos into Joy by Resolving Hidden Emotions

Hitting rock bottom is one of life's toughest challenges. When you find yourself there, you must remain in despair or conquer your fears. Imagine being overwhelmed by your current predicament. Look around and acknowledge that others may very well be in similar situations. You have already overcome much chaos and felt the triumph of discovering strengths you didn't know you had. Yet here you are again, at a critical juncture where the way forward seems unclear. Why? Because you've lost faith in yourself, or perhaps a past trauma, too painful to face then, has resurfaced.

The first path is one of surrender to fear and unresolved emotions, allowing them to turn your enthusiasm for life into dread. This path keeps you stuck, mired in negativity and despair. But there's another way—a path of growth and renewal. This path invites you to learn, accept, and creatively find solutions, becoming resourceful in adversity. The key to this transformative journey is to face and let go of those hidden emotions rather than burying them.

Emotional Paralysis vs. Creative Motivation

When we choose the path of emotional paralysis, we allow our unresolved emotions to dominate our thoughts and actions. Fear, doubt, and anxiety can become overwhelming, creating a mental and emotional fog that obscures our vision of the future.

Emotional paralysis manifests as:

1. Inaction: We become stuck, unable to make decisions or take steps forward. The fear of failure or the pain of past experiences prevents us from moving ahead.
2. Negative Self-Talk: Our inner dialogue becomes critical and defeatist, reinforcing feelings of inadequacy and hopelessness.
3. Isolation: We withdraw from others, believing no one can understand our struggles or offer meaningful support.
4. Loss of Enthusiasm: Our joy and passion for life diminishes, replaced by a pervasive sense of dread and resignation.

In contrast, choosing the path of creative motivation transforms how we respond to life's challenges. We tap into a wellspring of resilience and innovation by confronting our emotions and seeking innovative solutions. Creative motivation involves:

1. Acceptance: We acknowledge our emotions without judgment, understanding that they are a natural part of our human experience.
2. Resourcefulness: We explore new ways to address our challenges, drawing on our inner strengths and external resources.
3. Positive Self-Talk: We cultivate a supportive inner dialogue, encouraging ourselves with affirmations of our capabilities and potential.
4. Connection: We reach out to others, building a network of support and inspiration that fosters collective growth.
5. Renewed Enthusiasm: By engaging with our emotions and finding creative solutions, we rekindle our passion for life, embracing each day with purpose and excitement.

The Journey of Martie Smith: A Creative Chaos Warrior

My life has been a whirlwind of self-made dramas, unresolved traumas, and an adventurous search for passion, purpose, and mission. Growing up, I was an insecure little girl yearning for familial love that seemed perpetually out of reach. This lack of love left a void filled with self-doubt and fear.

For years, I was a wanderer, moving from place to place, job to job, searching for something to fill my emptiness. My adventures took me across different cultures and languages, and while they enriched my life, they also highlighted my inner turmoil. I battled with my insecurities, often creating dramas that only added to my emotional burden.

Yet, amidst this chaos, I discovered something profound. Each experience, no matter how tumultuous, was a stepping stone toward self-realization. I began to see the treasures in my journey—the blessings disguised as challenges and lessons hidden within my struggles.

It wasn't an overnight transformation. It was a gradual awakening, a realization that the creative little girl within me, who felt unloved and insecure, was a wellspring of potential and resilience. I found my true purpose by confronting my unresolved traumas and embracing my adventures. I learned to see my life's journey not as a series of missteps but as an epic tale of growth and transformation.

This transformation turned me into a Creative Chaos Warrior. I learned to harness the chaos around me, using it as a source of creativity and strength. I found peace in my heart and a renewed sense of purpose. My life became a testament to the power of resilience, the beauty of embracing one's journey, and the transformative power of facing one's fears head-on.

My story is a beacon of hope, reminding me that no matter how lost or broken you may feel, there is always a path to healing and growth. How can I overcome my past and find my true purpose? Embrace your journey, face your emotions, and let the Creative Chaos Warrior within you emerge. The choice is yours, and the results can paralyze or motivate you. Choose to be inspired, grow, and let your light shine brightly for all the world to see.

Our minds store everything, and unresolved emotions can weigh us down. But our memory bank isn't just a repository for pain. It also holds treasures: precious moments, unforgettable experiences, and once-in-a-lifetime events. These memories, when acknowledged and cherished, can transform our emotional landscape.

Life is dynamic and constantly changing, whether we know it or not. We must actively engage with all aspects of our experiences to etch those jewels of time into our hearts, allowing emotions to flow freely. Emotions are the key to blooming love, hope, forgiveness, and determination. Facing them head-on, instead of burying them, allows us to heal and grow.

Ignoring unresolved emotions often leads to a cycle of stress, doubt, negativity, and depression. It's easy to get stuck in this misery, feeling like there's no way out. But consider this: You've already overcome so much. The strength and resilience you discovered in past challenges are still within you. By acknowledging and confronting your emotions, you can break free from the cycle of despair and choose the path of growth and renewal.

Imagine the impact of fully engaging with your life, recognizing the actuality of your reality rather than living by preconceived notions formed by limited thoughts and past traumas. When we confront our emotions, we unlock the potential for true healing and renewal. This process isn't easy, but it's profoundly transformative.

Take a moment to examine your life. Reflect on the difference between your reality and the fears or limitations you've allowed to define you. You open the door to a life filled with genuine enthusiasm and purpose by facing your emotions. You start to see options and opportunities previously hidden by fear and doubt.

So, stand tall at this critical point in your life. Respect the journey you've been on, and trust in your ability to navigate through this moment. Embrace your painful and joyful emotions, and let them guide you toward a life filled with love, hope, and renewed determination. The path to healing and growth lies in facing your emotions as they appear, transforming your perspective, and igniting a genuine enthusiasm for life.

And that, my friend, is how I became a Creative Chaos Warrior. The choice is yours, but the results may paralyze or motivate you.

Creative Chaos Warrior

Discover the power of resilience and creativity with Creative Chaos Warrior. This book is your guide to embracing life's challenges and transforming them into opportunities for growth and empowerment. Take the first step today to unlock your potential, harness your creative spirit, and join a community of like-minded individuals who are turning their chaos into strength.

Become a part of the Creative Chaos Warrior movement. Share your story, connect with others, and be inspired to live boldly and resiliently. Let's turn our challenges into our greatest victories together!

To learn more about Martie, visit her website: http://martiemsmith.com/

About the Author

Martie Smith, an international award-winning author and Airforce Veteran was born in Colombia, South America, and has moved 49 times in her lifetime. She has learned many life lessons from different cultures, surgeries, and traumas. Now residing in North Carolina alongside her husband and partner of 40 years, she decided to share these tips to live a purpose-driven life journey with flexibility and resilience.

Martie has rebuilt and transformed her life and adopted a mission and vision to leave a legacy of hope for those open to implementing her helpful tips. They have come in handy for her to live a vibrant and joyful life now. The people who learn from her see her as an example that others want to follow and be inspired.

LinkedIn:
http://linkedin.com/in/martie-smith-8b062025

Facebook:
https://www.facebook.com/martie.smith.37?mibextid=qWsEUC

Instagram:
https://www.threads.net/@vinnersary

Website:
http://martiemsmith.com/